Colors of
JAPAN

by Holly Littlefield
illustrations by Helen Byers

COLORS OF THE WORLD

Carolrhoda Books, Inc. / Minneapolis

These illustrations are dedicated to Margaret Forrant, with thanks to Ben Liestman for the paper crane

Special thanks to Katherine A. Raskob and Kenichi Tazawa for their assistance in the preparation of this book

Calligraphy by Kenichi Tazawa
Map on page 3 by John Erste

This book is available in two editions:
Library binding by Carolrhoda Books, Inc.
Soft cover by First Avenue Editions
c/o The Lerner Publishing Group
241 First Avenue North
Minneapolis, MN 55401 U.S.A.

Library of Congress Cataloging-in-Publication Data

Littlefield, Holly.
  Colors of Japan / by Holly Littlefield ; illustrations by Helen Byers.
     p.   cm. – (Colors of the world)
  Includes index.
  Summary: Explores the different colors found in Japan's history, culture, and landscape.
  ISBN 0-87614-885-2 (lib. bdg.)
  ISBN 1-57505-215-6 (pbk.)
  1. Japan—Civilization—Juvenile literature. 2. Colors—Psychological aspects—Juvenile literature. 3. Symbolism of colors—Japan—Juvenile literature. [1. Japan. 2. Color.] I. Byers, Helen, ill. II. Title. III. Series.
DS821.L57   1997
952—dc21   96-44297

Manufactured in the United States of America
1 2 3 4 5 6 – SP – 02 01 00 99 98 97

Sea
of
Okhotsk

Hokkaido

Pacific
Ocean

Sea
of
Japan

Japan

Honshu

Mount
Fuji   Tokyo

Hiroshima

Shikoku

Kyushu

Mount
Aso

East
China
Sea

Introduction

Japan is a nation of ancient traditions, modern technology, and vivid colors. It is an archipelago, or a group of islands, linked together as one country. It lies off the coasts of Russia and North and South Korea in the Pacific Ocean. Japan's four main islands—Hokkaido, Honshu, Shikoku, and Kyushu—make up about ninety-five percent of the country, but there are also more than one thousand smaller islands. Altogether, Japan is about the size of the state of Montana. Japan's capital is Tokyo, one of the largest cities in the world.

The official language of Japan is Japanese. Even though written Japanese is made up of thousands of different symbols that are difficult to learn, nearly everyone in the country can read and write.

Red

 *aka* (ah-kah)

There is a solid **red** circle in the center of the Japanese flag. This circle represents the sun. The sun is an important symbol in Japan, a country that is sometimes known as the Land of the Rising Sun. In fact, the Japanese call their country Nippon or Nihon, which means "source of the sun." According to an ancient legend, the first emperor of Japan, Jimmu Tenno, was the great-great-grandson of Amaterasu, the sun goddess. At one time, all Japanese emperors claimed to be linked to the gods because they were direct descendants of Jimmu Tenno.

Black

 黒 *kuro* (koo-roh)

In ancient Japan, ninja warriors wore **black** so they wouldn't be seen at night. These warriors lived in hiding in the mountains, keeping their identities and training practices secret. Japan was ruled by rich, powerful families who were protected by warriors called samurai. Ninja were often the only people with the courage or ability to oppose samurai warriors.

Ninja practiced the martial art of ninjutsu, which means "the art of stealing in." Unlike other martial arts, such as karate or judo, ninjutsu had no one set of rules or moves. Instead, ninja were taught to use the fighting method that would work best for them in each battle. Ninja were also masters of disguise and experts with a variety of devices that helped them move about without being seen. Both men and women could be trained as ninja. The long training process started as soon as a child could walk.

Pink

ピンク *pinku* (peen-koo)

Every year, thousands of people turn out to admire the fragrant **pink** blossoms that cover cherry trees all over Japan. Cherry blossom season starts at the end of March in the southern part of the country and continues until the end of May in the north. The appearance of these pink blossoms signals the arrival of spring.

Cherry blossoms are the national flower of Japan. They are often used in *ikebana,* the Japanese art of flower arranging. *Ikebana* arrangements are simple, natural, uncluttered, and very beautiful. Cherry blossoms were also important to the samurai, powerful warriors from Japan's past who pledged their loyalty to one master. A samurai's honor mattered more to him than his life. In fact, samurai were expected to kill themselves rather than accept defeat or dishonor. These warriors saw the cherry blossoms as natural symbols of their own lives—brilliant and beautiful, but very short-lived.

Tan
黄褐色 *kikashoku iro*
(kee-kah-shoh-koo ee-roh)

Traditional Japanese houses have **tan** *tatami* mats on the floors instead of carpeting. *Tatami* mats are made of straw and are soft and comfortable to walk on. The Japanese wouldn't walk on a *tatami* mat while wearing shoes, however, that might get the mat dirty. People always leave their shoes by the front door and wear slippers while inside.

Tatami mats are always the same size, three feet wide by six feet long. The Japanese usually describe the size of their rooms by saying how many *tatami* mats they would hold. A small room might be a two-mat room, while a bigger one might hold eight mats. Japanese houses are usually very small. Sometimes rooms are divided by sliding doors or walls made of thick paper. The same room is often used for many different purposes. For example, during the daytime, a family might use their main room for eating, studying, and playing. Then at night, the family spreads out soft mattresses called futons on the *tatami* mats, and the main room becomes a bedroom.

Green

緑色 *midori iro* (mee-doh-ree ee-roh)

Green tea is used in the Japanese tea ceremony, which is over five hundred years old. The four basic principles of the tea ceremony are harmony, respect, purity, and tranquility. The ceremony is performed by a tea host, who is usually a woman. First the host and guests bow to each other to show respect. Then the host carefully cleans and purifies the utensils to be used and begins to make the tea. Everything is done very slowly and quietly while the guests watch. The sound of the water gently boiling over a small charcoal burner adds to the tranquility of the atmosphere. The host gives each guest a small, sweet cookie to eat, then she carefully, respectfully hands each person a small bowl of tea to drink. The sweet cookie helps to lessen the bitterness of the tea. Sometimes other food is served as well. The entire ceremony can take two hours or more, giving the guests time for quiet thought. Finally, the guests and host bow to each other again to end the ceremony.

White

白 *shiro* **(shee-roh)**

The subways in Tokyo, Japan's capital and largest city, are so crowded that during rush hour, special subway workers wearing **white** gloves are employed to push people into the cars before the doors close. These "pushers in," as they are called, try to be as polite and respectful as possible, but they have to get everyone into the cars quickly so the trains will run on time. The subways are so crowded that sometimes people's shoes fall off and can't be found. The windows on some of the cars have even been known to pop out from the pressure of so many passengers.

With a population of more than 125 million, Japan has more people than nearly any other nation in the world, but the actual area of the country is very small. Imagine trying to fit half the people of the United States into an area the size of Montana, and you will see why the Japanese have had to learn how to live close together.

14

Yellow

黄色 *kiiro* (kee-roh)

Some schools in Japan require that their young students wear a bright **yellow** cap as part of their school uniform. The yellow caps are worn for safety. They make it easier for drivers to see small children who are walking to school.

Education is extremely important to the Japanese, and most Japanese students are under a great deal of pressure to study hard and do well. The school year begins in April and ends in March. Children go to school Monday through Friday plus a half day on Saturday. On the average, Japanese students do about four times more homework than American students. Many Japanese students also go to special evening cram schools called *juku* to help them pass important tests.

17

Blue

青 *ao* (ah-oh)

The four main islands of Japan are surrounded by the **blue** waters of the Pacific Ocean on the east, the Sea of Okhotsk on the north, the Sea of Japan on the west, and the East China Sea on the south. These waters supply Japan with much of its food. The Japanese harvest and eat more fish and other food from the sea than the people of any other country in the world. Tuna, cod, sardines, shrimp, and even octopus, seaweed, and eel are often part of Japanese meals. Sometimes the seafood is served raw and sometimes it is cooked. No matter how it is prepared, seafood is usually served with rice.

Pearls, which are made by oysters, are another important product of the waters surrounding Japan. Before special pearl farming methods were developed, pearls were extremely rare. Japanese women called *ama* would dive to the ocean floor looking for oysters. The *ama* used no special diving equipment, but because of years of training and practice, they could hold their breath for as long as five minutes at a time. Sometimes they would bring up a thousand oysters before finding even one pearl.

19

Orange

オレンジ色 *orenji iro* (oh-rehn-jee ee-roh)

Japan has many active volcanoes, which frequently erupt, sending bright **orange** liquid rock called lava down their sides. Japan lies on one of the largest faults on Earth. This means that deep underground, huge pieces of the earth, called plates, are shifting and bumping into one another. The movement of these plates often causes volcanic eruptions and earthquakes on the earth's surface. More than one-tenth of all the active volcanoes in the world are in Japan. They are part of the Ring of Fire, a chain of volcanoes found throughout the Pacific Ocean. The tallest mountain in Japan is an inactive volcano called Fujiyama, or Mount Fuji. It last erupted in 1707. One of the biggest active volcanoes in the world—Mount Aso—is also located in Japan. Its crater is over fifteen miles wide. This volcano has erupted more than a hundred times in the last thousand years.

Gray
灰色 *hai iro* (hi ee-roh)

The crumbling **gray** walls of a bombed building stand in the Peace Memorial Park in Hiroshima, Japan. The building, called the Atomic Dome, has been left unrepaired as a reminder of the terrible power of nuclear weapons. In 1945 the United States dropped an atomic bomb on Hiroshima to bring World War II to an end. More than 200,000 people were killed either by the bomb itself or by the dangerous radiation that the bomb left behind.

Near the Atomic Dome stands a statue of Sadako Sasaki, a little girl who developed radiation sickness from the bomb. Sadako believed she would be cured if she could fold 1,000 paper cranes, because cranes symbolize happiness and long life to the Japanese. But she died after finishing her 964th crane. Every year, school children around the world send thousands of paper cranes to the Peace Memorial Park in memory of Sadako and all the other children who died at Hiroshima. The cranes represent the hope that nuclear weapons will never be used again.

Index